Science Inquiry

IS IT A FOOD WEB OR A FOOD CHAIN?

by Emily Sohn

PEBBLE

a capstone imprint

Pebble Explore is published by Pebble, an imprint of Capstone.
1710 Roe Crest Drive
North Mankato, Minnesota 56003
www.capstonepub.com

Library of Congress Cataloging-in-Publication Data
Names: Sohn, Emily, author.
Title: Is it a food web or a food chain? / Emily Sohn.
Description: North Mankato, Minnesota : Pebble, [2022] | Series: Science inquiry | Includes bibliographical references and index. | Audience: Ages 5-8 | Audience: Grades 2-3 | Summary: "A seed falls from a plant. A mouse eats the seed. An owl eats the mouse. Each animal gets energy from its food. How does energy flow from one living thing to another? Let's investigate food chains and food webs!"— Provided by publisher.
Identifiers: LCCN 2021002819 (print) | LCCN 2021002820 (ebook) | ISBN 9781977131409 (hardcover) | ISBN 9781977132574 (paperback) | ISBN 9781977154460 (pdf) | ISBN 9781977156136 (kindle edition)
Subjects: LCSH: Food chains (Ecology)—Juvenile literature.
Classification: LCC QH541 .S6283 2022 (print) | LCC QH541 (ebook) | DDC 577/.16—dc23
LC record available at https://lccn.loc.gov/2021002819
LC ebook record available at https://lccn.loc.gov/2021002820

Image Credits
iStockphoto/SDI Productions, 27; Shutterstock: Angela Lock, 5, Choksawatdikorn, 25 (bottom), clarst5, 19 (b), Cornelius Krishna Tedjo, 14 (b), Craig Lambert Photography, 25 (bottom right), Deep OV, 6 (cat), 21 (top right), diamant24, 6 (mushrooms), DmitrySV, 12, Eric Isselee, 6 (bear), 7 (sparrow, owl, deer), 9 (left), 18 (right), 19 (top), 21 (top left)(middle right), 25 (tl)(tr), fotosunny, 23, Guillermo Mayorga, 17, irin-k, 7 (beetle), JIANG HONGYAN, 25 (t), Jim Cumming, 6 (fox), 21 (top middle), Kovalchuk Oleksandr, 6 (raspberries), 8 (t), 21 (bottom left), kzww, 7 (earthworm), Leksele, 25 (bl), Lotus Images, 7 (sunflower seeds), Martin Rudlof Photography, 1, 14 (t), Michiel de Wit, 19 (middle), 21 (middle left), Nature Clickz, 11, Petr Simon, 15, PHOTO BY LOLA, 13, Pixcasso, 29, PRANEE JIRAKITDACHAKUN, 7 (grass), Rawpixel.com, 7 (person), Richard Seeley, cover, Rudmer Zwerver, 6 (mouse), 9 (b), 21 (m), Tarpan, 25 (m), Veniamin Kraskov, 18 (l), 21 (br), yingtustocker, 7 (cricket), 8 (b), 9 (r)

Artistic elements: Shutterstock/balabolka

Editorial Credits
Editor: Erika L. Shores; Designers: Dina Her and Juliette Peters; Media Researcher: Kelly Garvin; Production Specialist: Tori Abraham

All internet sites appearing in back matter were available and accurate when this book was sent to press.

TABLE OF CONTENTS

Words in **bold** are in the glossary.

WHAT IS A FOOD CHAIN?

A bird lands on a feeder. It eats seeds. Now it can fly away. It can build a nest and care for its chicks. The seeds gave the bird energy. Animals eat food for energy. You need energy to breathe and move.

Energy moves through the living world. Think about the bird. It eats seeds, which give it energy. Then a bigger animal eats the bird. Now, the bigger animal has energy. This is a food chain. Food chains and food webs show how energy moves between plants, animals, and the sun.

Let's do an investigation! Gather
index cards or small pieces of paper.
Look at the photos on these pages.
Write each thing on its own card.
Make 10 cards with just an arrow [—>]
on them.

bear

berries

mushrooms

fox   **cat**   **mouse**

worm

beetle

grass

owl

seeds

bird

person

grasshopper

deer

How do living things get energy?
Make pairs with your cards. Start with
a plant. Next comes an arrow. Then,
choose an animal that eats that plant.

How many pairs can you make?
Now try to make a chain of three.
What is the longest chain you can
make? Which animals eat more than
one type of food?

Keep your cards close by. You will
look at them as you read this book.

WHERE DOES ENERGY COME FROM?

All living things need energy. The sun makes energy. Plants take in that solar energy and use it to grow. Plants are called **producers**. They make their own food. **Consumers** eat other things for energy.

How many producers can you find in your stack of cards? Which cards show consumers?

Animals that eat plants are called **herbivores**. They might eat leaves, seeds, fruit, flowers, or roots. When an herbivore eats a plant, it gets energy from the plant. It is the same energy that the plant made with help from the sun.

Herbivores come in many shapes and sizes. Many insects are herbivores. Plenty of big animals are as well. Cows, deer, elephants, and pandas are all herbivores. Find some herbivores in your stack of cards.

Some animals get energy by eating both plants and animals. They are called **omnivores**. Grizzly bears eat fish and berries. Chickens eat worms and seeds. Mice eat insects and fruit.

Owls, tigers, sharks, and most spiders are meat-eaters. Animals that eat only other animals are called **carnivores**. They often have to hunt for their food. Hunters are **predators**. The animals they eat are their **prey**. Do you see any predators or prey in your cards?

Food chains don't end when plants and animals die. **Decomposers** eat dead stuff. They eat fallen trees, dried-up leaves, and dead animals.

Some decomposers are tiny, such as bacteria. Others are bigger. Earthworms and millipedes eat dead things. Then they poop out **nutrients** into the soil that plants can use to grow.

HOW DO FOOD CHAINS BECOME WEBS?

Look at the cards you linked together at the start of the book. A food chain describes how energy moves from one living thing to another in a series. First comes a producer. Then comes a consumer and maybe more consumers after that.

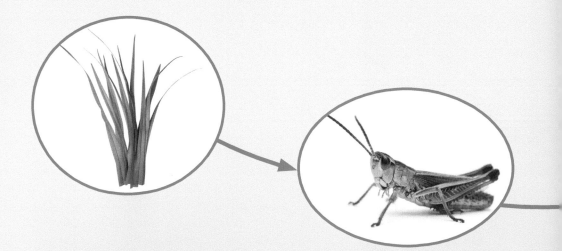

Can you see how a line of producers and consumers looks like a chain that is linked together? Each link depends on the next.

Mice are a part of many food chains. They eat lots of different foods. They eat fruit, seeds, meat, and more. And lots of animals eat them, like cats, snakes, and owls. If you put a bunch of food chains together, you get a food web. A food web may look like a spider web.

Look at your stack of cards. Can you make a web that shows chains crossing each other?

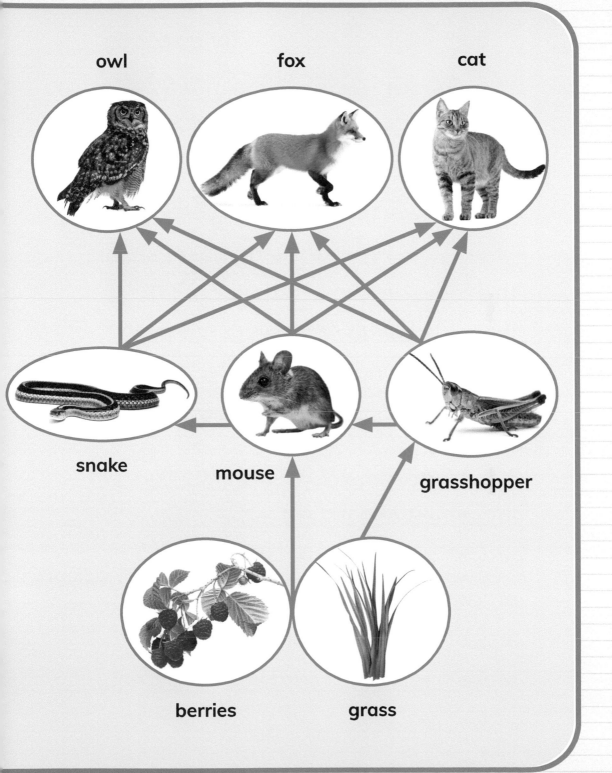

owl

fox

cat

snake

mouse

grasshopper

berries

grass

Owls and cats eat mice. But mice haven't disappeared. A healthy food web has balance. If the number of mice grows, the number of predators grows too. When mice numbers shrink, the same happens to their predators. If people cut down trees to put up buildings or hunt too many animals, they can change the balance.

Look at some of your animal cards. Imagine that you had more of each one. What would happen to its predators and prey? What if you had less of some and more of some others? Make a few extra cards and try it out.

There are food webs in every environment, not just on land. In the ocean, plankton and krill are tiny creatures. Krill eats the plankton. Next, krill is eaten by squid, seals, seagulls, and whales. Then the squid is eaten by seals, seagulls, and penguins.

Lakes, deserts, forests, and even cities have food webs. Can you see signs of any food webs out your window?

Ocean Food Web

squid

seal

seagull

krill

penguin

whale

plankton

HOW DO PEOPLE FIT INTO FOOD WEBS?

People are part of food webs. Eating gives you what you need to live and grow.

Draw a picture of a meal you ate recently. Label each type of food. List the ingredients in it. Can you figure out what kind of plants and animals each type of food came from?

Now look at your cards. Are any of them in the food webs you eat?

You have learned about the many ways that plants and animals are connected to each other and to the sun. Look at your cards again. Can you make any more chains or webs that you didn't make at the start of the book?

Try making some more cards of your own and adding them to your webs. Now, go outside and look for more animals and plants you can add. Food chains and food webs are all around you!

GLOSSARY

carnivore (KAHR-nuh-vohr)—an animal that eats only meat

consumer (kuhn-SOO-mur)—an animal that eats plants or other animals for energy

decomposer (dee-kuhm-PO-zur)—a living thing that turns dead things into food for others

energy (E-nuhr-jee)—the ability to do work

herbivore (HUR-buh-vor)—an animal that eats only plants

nutrient (NOO-tree-uhnt)—a part of food that is used for growth

omnivore (OM-nuh-vor)—an animal that eats both plants and other animals

predator (PRED-uh-tur)—an animal that hunts other animals for food

prey (PRAY)—an animal hunted by another animal for food

producer (pruh-DOO-ser)—a living thing that makes its own food

READ MORE

Hansen, Grace. *Food Chains.* Minneapolis: Abdo Kids, 2020.

Jacobson, Bray. *Food Chains and Webs.* New York: Gareth Stevens Publishing, 2020.

Ridley, Sarah. *Who Ate the Snake?: A Desert Food Chain.* New York: Crabtree Publishing Company, 2020.

INTERNET SITES

Food Chain and Food Web
ducksters.com/science/ecosystems/food_chain_and_web.php

Food Chain Facts for Kids
coolaboo.com/earth-science/food-chain-and-web/

INDEX